EDGE BOOKS

WAR MACHINES

INFANTRY FIGHTING VEHICLES

The M2A2 Bradleys

by Michael and Gladys Green

Capstone press

Mankato, Minnesota

Edge Books are published by Capstone Press
151 Good Counsel Drive, P.O. Box 669, Mankato, Minnesota 56002
www.capstonepress.com

Library of Congress Cataloging-in-Publication Data
Green, Michael, 1952–
    Infantry fighting vehicles: the M2A2 Bradleys / by Michael and Gladys Green.
    p. cm.—(Edge Books. War machines)
    Summary: Introduces the M2A2 Bradley, the United States Army's infantry
fighting vehicle, discussing its weapons, armor, role in combat as a troop carrier, and
future improvements.
    Includes bibliographical references and index.
    ISBN 0-7368-2415-4 (hardcover)
    1. M2 Bradley infantry fighting vehicle—Juvenile literature. [1. M2 Bradley
infantry fighting vehicle. 2. Armored vehicles, Military. 3. Vehicles, Military.]
I. Green, Gladys, 1954– II. Title. III. Series.
UG446.5.G689 2004
623.7'475—dc22   2003016062

Editorial Credits
Matt Doeden, editor; Jason Knudson, designer; Jo Miller, photo researcher

Capstone Press thanks Scott Gourley for his help in preparing this book.

Photo Credits
AP/Wide World Photos/Anja Niedringhaus, 7; Brennan Linsley, 19, 27;
    John Moore, 11
DVIC, 25
Getty Images Inc./Chung Sung-Jun, 16; Scott Nelson, cover
Michael Green, 9, 23
Photri-Microstock/Michael Green, 14–15
United Defense, L.P. , 5, 12, 21, 28

Table of Contents

CHAPTER 1

The M2A2 in Action

A group of U.S. Army soldiers slowly marches across the desert toward an enemy fort. The soldiers keep their distance. The U.S. soldiers worry about enemy soldiers shooting from the fort. They call for a unit of M2A2 Bradleys to clear the way.

A dozen Bradleys speed toward the fort. Enemy soldiers fire machine guns at the vehicles. But the bullets bounce off the Bradleys' thick armor.

LEARN ABOUT:

Troop carriers

Early Bradley models

General Omar Bradley

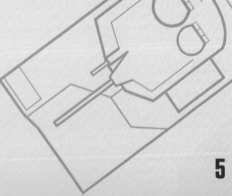

As the Bradleys approach the fort, enemy soldiers prepare to fire large antitank missiles at them. The Bradley crews quickly respond by targeting the missile launchers. In seconds, all of the enemy's antitank weapons are destroyed.

The Bradleys arrive at the fort unharmed. Large ramps drop from the rear of the vehicles. Seven heavily armed U.S. soldiers rush out of each vehicle. Before the enemy troops can react, the U.S. soldiers rush toward them and capture them. The fort is no longer a danger to the U.S. troops.

Soldiers exit the M2A2 from a rear ramp.

About the M2A2 Bradley

The M2A2 Bradley looks like a tank, but it is an infantry fighting vehicle. It is designed to carry soldiers to the battlefield. In combat, the Bradley often works alongside the Abrams main battle tank.

The original model of the Bradley was the M2A0. A company called United Defense built this vehicle for the Army in 1982. An improved model called the M2A1 entered service in 1986.

The first M2A2s entered Army service in 1988. The M2A2s have better armor and a more powerful engine than earlier models.

The M2A2 is part of the Bradley family. The other part is the M3A2 cavalry fighting vehicle. The M3A2 carries scouts instead of infantry. The Army has about 3,000 Bradleys in service.

The Bradleys are named for General Omar Bradley. General Bradley commanded U.S. Army units in World War II (1939–1945). He later served as the chairman of the U.S. Joint Chiefs of Staff.

The M2A1 was an earlier model of the Bradley.

CHAPTER 2

Inside the M2A2

The M2A2 Bradley weighs about 30 tons (27 metric tons). It is 21 feet, 2 inches (6.5 meters) long and 10 feet, 6 inches (3.2 meters) wide. It stands almost 9 feet, 9 inches (2.9 meters) tall.

The Body

The outer shell of the M2A2 is called the hull. It is made of an aluminum alloy. This mix of aluminum and other metals is 1.2 inches (3 centimeters) thick. Steel armor is added to the outside of the vehicle's hull. This armor adds extra protection from explosives and bullets.

The M2A2's hull is covered with metal armor.

LEARN ABOUT:

The hull

The diesel engine

Crew positions

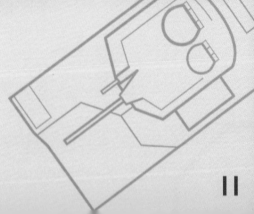

A turret sits on top of the hull. Two crew members operate the turret. They can point it in any direction. The main gun inside the turret can even point up and down.

Engine

The M2A2 has a powerful engine to keep up with the Army's tanks. A supercharged diesel engine provides this power. The engine produces up to 600 horsepower and allows the vehicle to reach speeds of 35 miles (56 kilometers) per hour.

The M2A2's engine burns large amounts of diesel fuel. The vehicle has a 175-gallon (662-liter) tank. The M2A2 can travel about 250 miles (400 kilometers) on a full tank. It can go only about 1.5 miles per gallon (.6 kilometers per liter) of fuel. Many cars can travel more than 30 miles per gallon (12.8 kilometers per liter) of fuel.

The M2A2

Function:	Infantry Fighting Vehicle
Manufacturer:	United Defense
Date First Deployed:	1988
Length:	21 feet, 2 inches (6.5 meters)
Height:	9 feet, 9 inches (2.9 meters)
Width:	10 feet, 6 inches (3.2 meters)
Weight Fully Armed:	30 tons (27 metric tons)
Engine:	Cummins VTA-903T turbo supercharged diesel
Top Speed:	35 miles (56 kilometers) per hour
Range:	250 miles (400 kilometers)

1 Armored hull

2 25 mm cannon

3 7.62 mm M240C
   machine gun

4 Tracks

5 Driver's hatch

6 Armored turret

7 TOW missile
   launcher

Tracks made of steel and rubber padding stretch around the M2A2's road wheels.

Tracks and Suspension

Each side of the M2A2 has six road wheels. A strip of steel and rubber padding called a track stretches around the wheels. The tracks allow the M2A2 to travel over rocky or uneven ground.

Each of the M2A2's wheels has an independent suspension system. The wheels can move up or down to stay on the ground. This system gives the M2A2 very good traction. It can travel over almost any surface.

Crew and Passengers

The M2A2 carries three crew members. The crew includes a vehicle commander, a gunner, and a driver. The crew members talk to each other through headphones built into their helmets.

The vehicle commander and the gunner sit inside the turret. Armored hatches cover their stations. They may leave the hatches open when not in combat. During combat, they close the hatches to stay safe from enemy fire. Soldiers call this action "buttoning up." When the hatches are closed, the crew members use periscopes and weapon sights to see outside.

The driver sits in the front of the hull. When the vehicle is buttoned up, the driver looks through four periscopes mounted to the hatch. The driver uses the Driver's Vision Enhancer (DVE) to see in darkness or in poor weather. The DVE creates pictures by detecting the heat from objects outside the vehicle.

Seven soldiers can ride in the back of the M2A2. They use a large rear ramp to enter and leave the vehicle. In older Bradley models, firing ports allowed soldiers to shoot from inside the vehicle. The M2A2 has no firing ports. It has extra side armor instead. Soldiers inside the vehicle can use periscopes to see outside.

Seven soldiers can ride in the back of the M2A2.

CHAPTER 3

Weapons and Tactics

The M2A2 Bradley has three main weapons systems. It carries a large automatic cannon, a machine gun, and an antitank missile-launching device. Crew members control all of these systems from the vehicle's turret.

Automatic Cannon

The 25 mm Bushmaster cannon is the M2A2's main gun. The Bushmaster is also called a chain gun. A small motor pulls a chain that feeds bullets into the gun. The chain holds up to 900 bullets.

The M2A2 crew can use several settings for the cannon. They can fire one shot at a time. They also can set the gun for automatic firing. This setting allows them to shoot either 100 or 200 rounds per minute.

The M2A2's main weapon is a 25 mm Bushmaster cannon.

LEARN ABOUT:

The 25 mm Bushmaster cannon

The M240C machine gun

Antitank missiles

The Bushmaster cannon is a very accurate weapon. Its mounting on the turret keeps it stable. It can easily track moving targets. It has a range of about 6,560 feet (2,000 meters). M2A2 crews can fire the cannon in any direction. They can even raise the turret to fire at helicopters and low-flying planes.

The Bushmaster cannon fires two main types of rounds. High-explosive (HE) rounds blow up on contact. Crews use HE rounds against targets such as trucks and groups of enemy soldiers. Armor-piercing discarding sabot (APDS) rounds are made to go through metal armor. Crews use APDS rounds against armored targets.

Machine Gun

The M2A2's turret also carries a 7.62 mm M240C machine gun. The M2A2's gunner uses this weapon against unarmored targets.

The M240C machine gun can fire
600 to 1,000 rounds per minute. It has a
range of about 3,935 feet (1,200 meters).
An M2A2 usually carries about 2,200
rounds of ammunition for this gun.

*The Bushmaster cannon
rotates with the turret.*

Missile Launcher

Cannons and machine guns cannot destroy enemy tanks. The M2A2 has an antitank missile launcher for this job. The launcher is attached to the vehicle's right side.

The missile launcher carries Tube-launched Optical Wire-guided (TOW) antitank missiles. The missiles have a range of more than 2 miles (3.2 kilometers). They carry explosive warheads that can go through 1 foot (30 centimeters) of steel. An M2A2 usually carries seven TOW missiles.

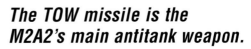

The TOW missile is the M2A2's main antitank weapon.

CHAPTER 4

The Future

Army officials have seen the value of the M2A2 in combat. M2A2s safely moved hundreds of troops during Operation Iraqi Freedom in 2003. The Army has an improved Bradley model called the M2A3 to continue this success.

The Army does not plan to build new M2A3s. Instead, it will upgrade the M2A2s it already has. In 1998, the Army received the first of these upgrades. The Army plans to upgrade 1,600 of the vehicles by 2009.

In 2003, the Army used the M2A3 in Iraq.

LEARN ABOUT:

The M2A3

Situational awareness

Equipment upgrades

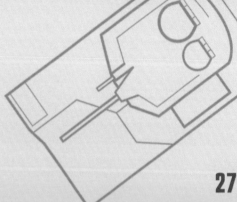

M2A3 Upgrades

The M2A3 Bradley looks almost identical to the earlier M2A2 version. But there are some important changes. Most of these changes help crew members know more about their surroundings. Crew members call this knowledge "situational awareness."

The M2A3 has new communications equipment and sensors. Its computers can connect with satellites in space. The satellite information helps crew members learn about enemy troops and terrain ahead.

The M2A3 also has an improved firing system. In older models of the Bradley, the gunner had to guess how far away a target was. The M2A3 sends out a laser beam to measure the distance to a target.

The M2A3 improvements help keep Bradley crews safe. M2A3 crews will be more effective in combat. The Army will continue to improve the Bradley to keep it useful for future missions.

The M2A3 is an improved model of the M2A2.

Glossary

horsepower (HORSS-pou-ur)—a unit for measuring an engine's power

hull (HULL)—the outside structure of a military vehicle that supports the other vehicle parts

periscope (PER-uh-skope)—a viewing device with mirrors at each end; M2A2 crew members use periscopes to view their surroundings while staying inside the vehicle.

sabot (sah-BOH)—a case that holds a round and fills up the extra space inside a gun's barrel

satellite (SAT-uh-lite)—a spacecraft that orbits the Earth

suspension (suh-SPEN-shuhn)—a system of springs and shock absorbers that allows the M2A2's wheels to move up and down

track (TRACK)—a strip of steel covered with rubber padding; a track runs over the wheels of a tank or infantry fighting vehicle.

turret (TUR-it)—a rotating structure on top of an M2A2 that holds the main gun

Read More

Bartlett, Richard. *U.S. Army Fighting Vehicles.* U.S. Armed Forces. Chicago: Heinemann Library, 2003.

Green, Michael. *Main Battle Tanks: The M1A1 Abrams.* War Machines. Mankato, Minn.: Edge Books, 2004.

Sievert, Terri. *The U.S. Army at War.* On the Front Lines. Mankato, Minn. Capstone Press, 2002.

Useful Addresses

United Defense
P.O. Box 15512
York, PA 17405-1512

U.S. Army Public Affairs
Office of the Chief of Public Affairs
1500 Army Pentagon
Washington, DC 20310-1500

Internet Sites

FactHound offers a safe, fun way to find Internet sites related to this book. All of the sites on FactHound have been researched by our staff.

Here's how:

1. Visit *www.facthound.com*
2. Type in this special code **0736824154** for age-appropriate sites. Or enter a search word related to this book for a more general search.
3. Click on the **Fetch It** button.

FactHound will fetch the best sites for you!

Index